Deb's book

Illustrated by Nina O'Connell

The race page 2

The red house page 7

Up and down page 12

Nelson

The race

"Can you run fast?"
said Deb the rat.
"Let's have a race."

"I can run fast,"
said Ben the dog.
"But Pat the pig can't."

"I can run fast,"
said Jip the cat.
"But Pat the pig can't."

"I can run fast,"
said Sam the fox.
"But Pat the pig can't."

"I can run fast,"
said Pat the pig.
"Look at me."

The red house

"I have a pot of
red paint," said Deb.
"I want a red house.
But I am small and
the house is tall."

"I will help you," said Meg.
"But I am small and
the house is tall."

"I will help you," said Ben.
"But I am small and
the house is tall."

"I will help you," said Sam.

"I am tall."

"Your house is red and we are red."

Up and down

"Get on the see-saw, Meg," said Pat the pig.
"It will go up and down."

Meg got on the see-saw.
It did not go up and down.

"Get on the see-saw, Jip,"
said Pat the pig.
"It will go up and down."
But it did not go up and down.

"Get on the see-saw, Ben,"
said Pat the pig.
"It will go up and down."
But it did not go up and down.

"Get on the see-saw, Deb,"
said Pat the pig.
"It will go up and down."
Deb got on the see-saw.
It went up and down.